BLOOMING INTO LIFE:
AN ENERGY HEALING JOURNEY

Amanda Beth Johnson

Blooming Into Life

Amanda Beth Johnson

Bloomfield, IA

Amanda@AmandaBethHealing.com

Ordering Information:

Special discounts are available on quantity purchases by corporations, associations, educational institutions, and others. For details, contact Amanda Beth Johnson above.

Printed in the United States of America

First Edition

Softcover ISBN 978-8-9887-0580-2

Publisher

Winsome Entertainment Group LLC

Sandy, UT

Blooming Into Life:
an Energy Healing Journey

*"Healing may not be so much about getting better, as about letting
go of everything that isn't you - all of the expectations,
all of the beliefs - and becoming who you are."*
~Rachel Naomi Remen (2010)

*"Resilience is our ability to bounce back from life's challenges
and unforeseen difficulties, providing mental protection
from emotional and mental disorders."*
~Michael Rutter (1985)

*"Change the way you look at things...
and the things you look at will change."*
~Dr. Wayne Dyer

Thank You

I want to express my gratitude to so many individuals throughout my entire life. I thank each and every one of you for helping me on the path of my life. I appreciate the gifts of knowledge, struggle, and lessons each of you has contributed to my story and path. Knowing there is just one true path for my soul to reach enlightenment, I am a Be-ing of the Divine Light and Love.

My greatest gratitude goes to those of you who have helped shine a light on these factors—a shoutout from the rooftops to those who saw what I had forgotten within me. You tucked me under your wing, held my hand, and continued illuminating my path. You have stayed with me and helped me through the bumps and gullies. You have helped me to learn about vulnerability, growth, and ultimately my true potential.

CONTENTS

Chapter 1

Early Years with Careers and Volunteering Diversity

My family moved to what became my hometown in late 1973. My mother and stepfather relocated here to start and manage the first ambulance service in Davis County. Before this, the funeral home was the only option for transportation.

My mom worked at the local nursing home and later became an RN. She spent many years as the intensive care unit (ICU) night supervisor at our county hospital. She challenged the paramedic test as a registered nurse. She became the 118th paramedic in the state. My stepfather, the ambulance service manager, also became certified as a paramedic.

Iowa has the famous RAGBRAI bike ride. (Register's Annual Great Bike Ride Across Iowa, named for the Des Moines Register newspaper.) My dad and his boss were the first medical staff for this prestigious bike ride across Iowa. It is a tremendously respected annual event, a first of its kind that has continued for over fifty years. My parents would attend each year as medical staff—this was their idea of vacation! My grandmother would come and care for my brother and me. My brother was a sleepwalker—we learned when Grandma witnessed him walking down the driveway!

My parents always had grand stories of all the shenanigans on RAGBRAI. I just knew I had to be a part of that! I was never athletic. While I rode my ten-speed Hiawatha bike everywhere, I would never become conditioned to ride amongst the athletes and pros on this ride. To this day, people around the globe await the much-anticipated release of the route in January. The ride has become so popular that it has limited openings: 15,000–20,000 riders per day.

WHAT IS RAGBRAI ALL ABOUT? (Quoted from The Des Moines Register website)

RAGBRAI, The Register's Annual Great Bicycle Ride Across Iowa, is an annual seven-day bicycle ride across the state. In its 50th year, RAGBRAI is the oldest, largest, and longest recreational bicycle touring event in the world.

This rolling celebration of Iowa attracts participants from all 50 states and many foreign countries. It has covered thousands of miles through the years, and hundreds of thousands of riders have hopped in the saddle to pedal part of those miles.

RAGBRAI is a bicycle ride, not a race. It started in 1973 as a six-day ride across the state of Iowa by two Des Moines Register columnists who invited a few friends along. It is held the last full week in July. RAGBRAI is planned and coordinated by The Des Moines Register. Riders who participate in RAGBRAI understand that they do so at their own risk.

The RAGBRAI route averages 468 miles and is not necessarily flat. It begins somewhere along Iowa's western border on the Missouri River and ends along the eastern border on the Mississippi River.

Eight Iowa communities along the RAGBRAI route serve as "host" communities for overnight stays. RAGBRAI is a guest in these communities, and we ask our riders to behave as such.

The people of Iowa truly make RAGBRAI the special event that it is by opening up their towns and communities to participants. We hope you can enjoy this Iowa hospitality and join us for a memorable trip across the state.

So, to be a part of this grand adventure, RAGBRAI, I would need to become an EMT (emergency medical technician).

My parents divorced when I was three years old. Mom returned to Iowa and later married my stepdad. I struggled with fitting in at school. I struggled academically and socially, yet excelled in art and things I did on my own. Friends were limited, primarily to the extent of the neighborhood kids and my brother, who was six years younger than me.

With divorced parents several states apart, I had a visitation schedule. Summers and between Christmas and New Years were spent with my father. He had remarried, and my stepmother did not work outside the home. Life there was alluring to be an only child doing all the seasonal fun things—the zoo, sea world, family picnics, and gatherings.

It all sounded and felt refreshing, so after the end of sixth grade, I left my mom's with no intention of returning in the fall.

Life did not go as "sugarcoated" as promised after moving to greener pastures. My move to Ohio quickly became the family's move to Mississippi, and I was no longer the only child. My brother's adoption was finalized, and a half brother was on the way. The move to the South was for my father to take a sales job. This job did not fulfill the promises. The family returned to Ohio within two years when that company went under. Returning to Ohio became the fourth different school I had attended in four consecutive years.

Many of my academic struggles were blamed on the frequent moves in school. Family life was another significant factor. I returned back to my mom's in Iowa. At first, I did not want to return to the local school. Classmates and locals had been less than receptive toward me when I came home for summer visitation since moving away.

I returned to my hometown high school in the middle of my junior year. Being a significantly smaller high school, I had few courses to choose from. I spent a lot of my time in the art room. Oil painting was my favorite thing to do. My classmates dubbed me "Flying Needle" in our fiber arts class. I was not allowed to do any cooking in the home ec class—I coached my classmates. I was raised with many basic living skills of cleaning, cooking, sewing, and other needlework the teacher felt it was an unfair advantage in the classroom.

My mom was a single parent at this point. She now managed the ambulance service, worked at the hospital, and had returned to college to become a doctor.

There I was, bored to tears in high school, so I enrolled in the local community college's basic emergency medical technician (EMT) class. A couple of other gals with the ambulance service took it with me. I did my night school homework during my high school study halls. It disgusted my classmates—that was where I learned that we learn best by teaching. I reinforced my learning by "teaching/explaining" to high school classmates in study hall.

I was still seventeen when the course was over. I had to wait to turn eighteen to sit for the state certification exam. My early practice with the mannequins as part of an EMS family showed when it came to producing perfect strips in my basic EMT class. The mannequins of the day generated a paper "strip" to show the effectiveness of the CPR (cardiopulmonary resuscitation) performed, the depth of the compressions and breaths, as well as the timing or rate. Another classmate, who was struggling, offered to pay me for mine. I don't think so!

I graduated high school, sat for my state level EMT test, and was certified that summer when I turned eighteen. I continued to work for the local ambulance service. My EMT certification was a huge leg up when I went to college. Instantly, the ambulance service in the college town hired me! The following summer, after my first year of college, I took the advanced EMT training to become a Level 1 EMT in Iowa. The next level, at the time, was paramedic. A Level 1 had advanced skills in IV starting, intubation, and defibrillation added to that. I was an EMT-ID by the time I was nineteen. And most importantly, I could be a part of the RAGBRAI medical staff. I was on the medical staff for three out of five years. It became my annual vacation too.

Hard Work Is the Greatest Reward

I started my college career at the only school that would accept me due to my high school grades. School was a considerable challenge. One challenge was I had attended six different high schools before graduation. The struggle in college was far more than I ever imagined. My GPA would have made you think I was a party animal, though I was far from that. Those first years of college were met with many tears and much frustration.

I was proud to have already accomplished the status of being an EMT as I sat awkwardly at a school desk supporting my ever-trendy eighties fashion: white tennis shoes with red polka dots, and the clear jelly soles, topped with my jean jacket sporting buttons of all styles from seam to seam to hem. I guess it was the shoes…

A few days later, this guy knocked on my dorm room door. My RA had made the cutest construction paper names on our doors. The guy was Jeff. He was a nontraditional student who couldn't believe I was only a freshman because I was already an EMT, and he was just starting the class. Soon, we started dating (creating my first and only fake ID), cooking at his apartment, and having healthy debates on nearly every subject. He became my typist and study partner, although we didn't have the same classes. He was on an accounting track while I was a double major in biology and psychology, pursuing occupational therapy.

Jeff helped me locate the ideal college to better fit my educational goal of becoming an occupational therapist. That summer, we became engaged. I said, "Yes, when I graduate." I knew all the crucial lessons that

I "must have an education" before life began. My college credits counted, and my graduation was in sight; we announced our wedding date in the fall of 1991.

After relocating to Grand Forks, ND, and attending the University of ND, I began to learn how I learned. Being very distraught over my grades and my apparent inability to comprehend what I had read, I found myself huddled in a ball of tears under my desk one time too many. I didn't want to live. There was just no way I could be this much of a failure.

Somehow, I found myself in the hands of a counselor with the university's counseling services. After only a few sessions, the counselor referred me to disabled student services (DSS) at the university. It was there that I participated in what seemed like endless testing. They even got my records from when I was a sophomore in high school in Ohio. All of these tests confirmed that I was, in fact, dyslexic and dysgraphic.

This is where life got interesting. Initially, this diagnosis was an enormous challenge for me. I accepted tutoring and notetakers, and all of my textbooks were converted to cassette tape. I had a cassette player issued by the National Library Service for the Blind and Print Disabled since I was officially diagnosed. Some textbooks were unavailable on cassette through the library for the blind. Student volunteers in the DSS office recorded required textbooks to cassette tape for me. It was interesting to listen to the recordings of my physiology book. This reader misread many Latin abbreviations, which I had to correct each time in my brain. The biggest one was "mmHg," which is millimeters of mercury, referring to how blood pressure is read in this context.

My life was saved with the endless support of the University of North Dakota DSS office. I earned better grades with these adaptive services. With dyslexia and dysgraphia, reading and writing were a significant challenge for me. Reading was not pleasurable; it was a challenge. I would listen to my textbooks and follow along with the physical book in front of me, and luckily, I was able to pay attention and comprehend what it was. Identifying that I am a verbal learner, the DSS staff also read my tests to me. In my first year of college, my GPA was 1.12. In my last and fourth year of college, carrying twenty and twenty-two credits (twelve credits were considered full-time status) in the fall and spring semesters, I graduated with a 3.75 GPA.

I'm very proud of the work I can do with adaptations. The key was learning that I needed the adaptations and being pointed in the right direction to utilize and accept them. The idea of returning to college and completing a master's level program would be very daunting if it did not have the appropriate support services I had before.

My beginning in EMS supported my efforts through college. I completed my bachelor's in psychology with minors in rehabilitation and gerontology. Look out, human services—here I come!

My First Human Services Job

Jeff skillfully crafted two resumes for me. One resume to target my favorite population: geriatrics. In 1991, even a minor in gerontology was a rare thing. The second resume was a more general resume to cover general social work careers.

I recall the most intimidating interview I had ever experienced. I was wearing a skirt, heels, and pantyhose, and sitting at the end of a long boardroom table. Four or five men in business suits interviewed me. The intimidation was more because I was positioned at the head of the table. I wondered how I fit into this arena—a downtown Utica, New York, boardroom. I was overwhelmed, having lived all of my life in the great, chill Midwest. I will never forget the drips of pure anxious sweat running down my back. Oh wait, they started talking about start dates! But I needed time off a few weeks later to be medical staff on RAGBRAI. It had become my annual vacation. I didn't want to lose my first full-time real job by requesting time off before I started. I had been on that ride many times and looked forward to many more. I was hired and granted the time off.

This first job was part of the pilot program of the Homebuilders model out of Washington State. It was full-on crisis based. Families could accept this in-home crisis service within twenty-four hours or lose their children to foster care placement within forty-eight hours. The premise was that a crisis is an opportunity for change. We were in a short-term, high-intensive program, and worked on a team of five.

We met families where they were functioning. I learned basic plumbing skills and met many challenges head-on. We worked on and in every aspect of a given family's life. The outcome was to have better equipped parents providing the best opportunity for their children in a safe and secure environment. I also gained considerable insight into the family court system. I was learning valuable lessons about testifying and courtroom formalities.

Compassion for Others

There was so much training to meet the program's needs and follow the core beliefs. We were a team of fresh college graduates with no preconceived ideas about how everything worked. Our supervisor was a therapist with a specialty in suicidology. That alone was fascinating.

They sent us off to train about an hour away from the office. A newly formed team of four college graduates, a fifth would join the team later in the program. Of course, our supervisor attended this training as well. It allowed our team to connect and create a bond, and to be at the forefront of a new way of thinking and working to prevent foster care placement. I was so out of my element, having grown up in a small Midwest town, about to be sent out to the projects of Utica, New York, and save the world.

I was hired for a crisis intervention program, with no cell phones, just pagers and pay phones. There was twenty-four-hour availability for the families we served for six to eight weeks. The "crisis is the opportunity for a change" was at the core of this program.

I learned early on that my keen powers of observation did not have a place in most neighborhoods where I worked. Attention and focus would remain only on my assigned family and those interacting directly with them.

Working in the inner city, our employer had great trainings from the local law enforcement regarding personal safety and how to respond and react in such a manner to be defensive and not get into bad situations in the first place. The running joke at training was that we would all be issued bulletproof sleeping bags and handguns. Seventy-five percent of our time was spent directly with the families in their homes.

Our positions allowed us to dress casually. Jeans and T-shirts were often the most appropriate. Sometimes we did minor home repairs. The toilet was the thing most often in need of repair. Each family had a stipend we could access to make necessary repairs to increase the home's overall safety for the children.

With our random work hours, casual dress code, and need to access the office after hours, the agency placed us in an office space at the YMCA in downtown Utica. Our office would be available after hours as the men's shelter was also there. Our paths did not often cross, and it was yet another uniqueness to my first experiences away from my Midwestern roots.

Adapting readily and accepting a family wherever they were was crucial for being welcomed into their home. A few years later, I became the Runaway and Homeless Youth Program director. With this program, I certified families willing to host runaway children as they navigated through the system and reunited with their families safely and securely. I was already all too familiar with the family court system for my previous job, and now I learned the extensive rules and laws for runaway and homeless youth, as well as emancipation—all in a time without Google or the internet.

The runaway job was yet another example of on-the-job training. When I interviewed for the job, I was unaware of the scope of laws regarding runaway and homeless youth—the peculiarities in state and federal laws and where the precedence lay. I had to be a quick study! There was a federal audit of the program just two to three months after I took the position. I certified some great families to care for the youth who could not continue to reside in their own homes. We were fortunate to have these host families for the kids to reach out to for reassurance. Many remained advocates for the child after their stay.

Helping the youth to work through issues and find safe havens was truly rewarding. Providing counseling and teaching life skills were my primary focus after securing safe housing. Most often, we reunited the families. Always having emergency supplies for a child and a safe place for them to stay in or near their school district kept me on my toes. Creating that safe environment with understanding and counseling in place was a heartfelt experience. Many only needed to know they could reach out and talk. We were providing interventions to prevent this from happening frequently too. We all need to be heard. I had a staff of three caseworkers to supervise in this program.

I later worked for the County Council on Alcoholism and Substance Abuse, developing an Employee Assistance Program (EAP) focusing on parenting skills. These sessions would be held in the office—a massive change from my other jobs. I genuinely enjoy working with people in their home environment rather than in the office. Most people can "make nice" and behave in an office for forty-five minutes to an hour. However, seeing how a family functions in their home truly allows you a vantage point in being able to assess and assist them in making progress.

Life Uprooted

In the fall of 1996, Jeffrey was killed in a motor vehicle crash less than three miles from our home. We belonged to a local car club with our classic car. I was the secretary/treasurer and behind on the minutes for the upcoming meeting, so I was not in the car with him that morning as we had planned. As a bizarre string of events, I was at the crash scene before his body was removed. I was escorted home by highway patrol, who stayed until someone could arrive to be with me.

So many of our experiences came together in these moments of his death and the decisions I, as a twenty-seven-year-old, would be forced to make. Jeff's part in typing all my college stuff allowed us healthy debates—particularly the "death and dying" classes lending to discussing our beliefs.

My world was beyond rocked. Decisions needed to be made: my husband, my partner, my everything gone. I was totally alone. My job was part time, I lived in an extremely rural area, and the winters were nothing I could do alone where we had chosen to live.

Following Jeffrey's death, I relocated back to Iowa. After dealing with my grief, not always effectively, I returned to the workforce. I revised my two distinct resumes. I worked a short time in my mother's medical office to reacclimate myself into returning to the workforce.

Getting back into the workforce was a significant struggle. Employers were more concerned about the time I had taken between jobs. When they learned I had taken time for a personal loss, they passed judgment and thought I was now damaged goods. During one interview, I was asked why I came from a supervisory position to seek line staff work. At this time in the interview, I felt my fate was sealed against me. I answered candidly: "I have no desire to be in a supervisory role after my loss and relocation." I was offered the position on the spot. I was so happy to be working again. I didn't haggle on the salary!

I finally landed a job back with a family crisis program. While this program was loosely based on the Homebuilders model, it had many familiarities. I enjoyed working in the family's home once again, making a difference using "crisis as an opportunity" for change and growth.

Volunteering Through My Livelihood

My first memory was volunteering at the local nursing home as a child, visiting residents, writing letters, or sewing name tags on new clothing. Oh, that was a day. I was nine and sitting just inside the door to Lila's room to sew her name labels on the largest boxed brassieres I had ever encountered! Sitting at her doorway allowed the entire world passing by to see this. I enjoyed spending time with the residents as much as they enjoyed the opportunity to visit.

While living in Grand Forks, North Dakota, for college, I became acquainted with the American Red Cross (ARC). I was first a shelter nurse during the floods of 1989. Jeff had his Boy Scout troop volunteer to fill sandbags, and that was the start of our connection to the ARC. Jeff and I became members of the Disaster Assistance Team (DAT), working with families after natural disasters and fires and providing them with emergency shelter, food, and clothing. I also began teaching first aid and CPR for the Red Cross chapter in Grand Forks. I volunteered with the American Red Cross in three states for thirty years.

When Jeff and I moved to Upstate New York, I became involved in the local hospice. Many of the hospice patients I worked with did not have a lot of family. My patients were unique and taught me so much about life and living.

Returning to Iowa had me volunteering with several organizations, including 4-H, and the Council for Prevention of Child Abuse and Neglect. Of course, with my children, I also volunteered with the school, music boosters, chaperoning, and dance studios, including costume design and sewing—everything from creating three-dimensional costumes to emergency backstage repairs of dance shoes and outfits. As a dance mom, I always had Band-Aids, needles and thread, and safety pins at all times!

Volunteering was significantly rewarding as I met with so many different individuals at so many spectrums and times in their lives and met their needs as they presented. Volunteering these days has more to do with community and networking engagements and the Master Gardener program. I love the educational side of Master Gardeners.

A Pattern to My Life

Yes, there's a pattern here. I was making myself available to others within their time frame and working many of my jobs as crisis response. Being on call 24/7, even when it wasn't my turn to carry the pager, I was still available to my coworkers to answer any questions they might have if a crisis arose with a family I was assigned—that role of always being available carried into my role as supervisor for the various programs too. I enjoy working with people to make a change and to make a difference. Being open at their darkest times is rewarding on its own.

Listening is the biggest key to hearing what people need. My supervisor, the very first one, the suicidologist, taught us about empathic listening. I was listening for the words clients did not say. Listening for the things that people do not talk about, hearing them for what they say and acknowledging where they are, and recognizing how they feel and what they need to get through the day is vital. I learned that we are human beings, all completely different. We are just as unique as snowflakes. To assume that anyone sees anything the way I do is entirely wrong. It was my duty to, first and foremost, understand how they were seeing what they were seeing and to understand why. Only then could I provide any assistance to help them meet the end goal—their goal!

When you think about it, what makes you awesome?

List 20 things that make you awesome and unique using the acronym SAAVE.

Skill set: The combination of knowledge, personal qualities, and abilities you've developed through life and work.

Activities you enjoy outside of work.

Appearance: What are you confident about?

Values that are important to you.

Eat: What do you like to eat that is unique to you?

Reflecting on your many great qualities allows you to better connect with your greatest inner qualities.

Chapter 2

Stampede Graphics and Helping Business Owners Grow

Plot Twist!

Seven years back in Iowa, I had seen many personal changes. I bought a house, got married, had a bonus daughter, and had another child on the way. While I truly loved helping others, I knew my family must come first. I needed a job or path that would allow me to be available after school and on weekends. All of my previous jobs did not allow this consistently. I knew I could not leave a newborn in someone's care while I left to care for other families.

I had brief thoughts of returning to school. I completed my BS degree in psychology and two minors within the traditional four years. I had most of the anatomy, physiology, and biology classes I would need to complete a master's in nursing quickly. That would have good pay, regular hours, and benefits. But going back to school? Oh, I was not sold on that idea. Would a nursing program have a DSS? Would they understand my needs? I was still determining where I wanted to take a new career. I would also be leaving my newborn in someone's care to attend classes; how was that different from leaving them for work?

Thoughts of changing a career, needing further education, or not staying in human services were not any thoughts I had before becoming pregnant. I didn't know who this critter would be, but I knew I had to be there for this child. Conceiving was a challenging task. There were many tests, trials, and tribulations over the two years to conceive. This child was very planned. I made many changes in my diet and lifestyle activities to give this child the best opportunity to be healthy. After all this, I was only returning to full-time human services work if it fell within the constraints of traditional school hours.

My mom had grown her medical practice. She began doing cash-based, nontraditional procedures like Botox and permanent cosmetics. I was Johnny-on-the-spot. I helped her in these endeavors, including designing artwork, fliers, brochures, intake forms, and all the matching stationary she needed for her new branding. A local business had a sign in the window that read "Turnkey Business For Sale." To this day, I still see "*Turkey* Business." It was a sign business. My mother and her friend walked past the sign several times on their morning walks. She encouraged me to look into this as a career change. Who, me? A sign maker? She encouraged me by citing all of the signage and graphic designing I had done for her and how much I enjoyed doing it.

It was a Monday morning, and I gave the phone number a call. We met later that day and visited the owner's property, where a gooseneck trailer was. The trailer was a massive part of the business purchase price.

By Wednesday, I was at the bank. I initially went to the bank that held the mortgage on my home. However, because I was seeking to purchase a brick-and-mortar business in another community, the banker encouraged me to seek funding through a bank in my local community. Well, that was a silly proposition. I did it. I went to each and every bank in my small community. I was denied funding for purchasing this business because I did not have a formal education in graphic design. The local bankers did not feel that my desire to be successful, coupled with my many years of working with people, had any bearing in predicting my success at a new business.

I returned to the mortgage holder and received the funding to purchase within a week. The previous business owner agreed I would receive all the proceeds for the remaining month of business while in training. She would stay with me while finishing my old job to transition me into the business. I kept the business name and logo for continuity with existing customers.

The storefront could have been better used. The previous owner did far more selling on the road at horse and cattle shows and sales than in the storefront. It was a small store on the historic city square. There was a large desk, a tote or two of T-shirts, a wall rack of eight to ten rolls of vinyl, a box or two of aluminum sign blanks, and a folding banquet table. Of course, the shirt and hat heat presses had their cart with heat transfers stored underneath. The large trash barrel, and there you had it. The computer was on its last leg, and I was entrusted with the software "dongle key." Without this single little device inserted into the USB port, the software did not run.

Oh my, what had I done? I could have been more computer savvy. I had mastered Dragon Naturally Speaking to dictate my reports for my human service job. I could send and receive emails. I kept family members up to date on the milestones throughout my pregnancy. I had a child coming and wanted to be present and watch them grow. I wanted to spend more time with my oldest daughter as she began to go through many life changes herself. I wanted to be present. I wanted a closer sense of immediate family.

By the time I left my human services job, I had attained supervisory status after seven years. Due to that, I needed to provide three weeks of notice rather than two. However, the agency did not see continuing the program, so I provided them with five weeks of service before leaving.

I set to work to establish and maintain regular storefront hours. I'm not a morning person, so 10:00 a.m. worked fine for me. To have customers, I needed to either be there first thing in the morning before many people went to work or be available after they had gotten off work. So there you have it. My store hours were from 10:00 a.m. to 6:00 p.m., Monday through Friday. I had all my clipart books arranged and filed. I purchased more vector format clipart, all organized in sleeves and binders. I had display racks and methods of packaging decals that could be premade. Stampede Graphics was a new adventure!

The gooseneck trailer doubled as sleeping quarters. We removed a shower and portable commode to have more room for signs and supplies when we traveled. I was nearly seven months pregnant. This whole camping thing was probably not going to go well.

We occasionally continued to do on-site sign making following the previous owner's schedule. There was also a limited supply of T-shirts and transfers so people could have a new T-shirt at their event. The previous owner had been very horse and ranch centered. I took the business into another avenue. My husband was a semitruck driver. We rapidly received many orders to fulfill Department of Transportation (DOT) truck numbers. We also began lettering several trucks and fleets locally.

My husband was a fantastic partner in this business and applied the larger decals after his day's work or on weekends. Our oldest, at nine, helped as well. No more after-school daycare—she came to the shop. Sometimes she would help with the business when homework was complete. She loved to work on the computer and learn the software for school projects. She became a popular pick if lettering for a poster was needed.

Our new baby arrived, healthy in every aspect. She was an asset to our family. She went to work with me every day. I created an area in the storefront that was her area: all her toys, a pack-and-play for naps, and a wind-up swing.

In the beginning, while building this business, I recall people coming to me with their ideas. I would send them away for about twenty minutes or so and have their projects completed. Many of these people continued coming back to me for various needs. It was another leap of faith a year or two later when I realized that I needed other products to offer. We began designing business cards and brochures and creating wholesale accounts. We also began screen and pad printing for T-shirts and promotional items. Wow, that was a massive leap of faith and one of my best purchases.

So what does designing promotional marketing items, business cards, brochures, signs, and T-shirts have to do with helping people? I've always been helping people! Real simple: people would come to me with their crazy, harebrained ideas. They would have chicken scratches and pencil drawings, and sometimes it was only their description of what they were trying to accomplish. I would tell people I needed to sleep on it. My dreams have always been busy, animated, and full of color. My best ideas came to me while I slept. I could listen, feel, and see what someone was telling me. I could see in their mind's eye what they were looking for. I sold them what they needed, which was only sometimes what they asked for.

When people speak to me, I create three-dimensional models of everything in my brain. Back in the day, when I participated in juried craft shows, making teddy bears from fabric and recycled fur coats or cherished family heirlooms, I always knew exactly what they would look like. This conceptual vision was how I could strategically place the pattern to preserve the best features of the heirloom. Only recently have I understood that most people do not see things this way. Research has shown me that it concerns my dyslexia, which is how my brain puts things together.

I was able to create magic and help people grow their own business or side hustle. I also found myself doing some business coaching, watching new individuals come into owning their own business, reassuring them through the difficult times and, every once in a while, calling them to say, "Hey, how's it going?"

When I purchased the company, I remained in the rented storefront. The landlord announced the upcoming availability of more building space with the retirement of the barber who used the back portion.

The division of the building was odd. We shared a main entrance, and there was a long hallway to his small shop in the back. Jack was pushing ninety years old. Sometimes he seemed grumpy, but as my daughter toddled around the building, he always welcomed her. She would go to his shop and crawl into chairs to watch and socialize. Taking on that space would have been bittersweet. It would only add about 25% more space, and the rent would be twice its current amount. I knew I had to move. A local building was secured, and I could rent before purchasing the building.

Additionally, my daughter would have her play area. Her room would not be subject to the public. She could have her little TV, her VCR, and DVD player, as well as mounds and mounds of toys and crafts and all kinds of things to keep her busy and close to me. She had a 1950s vintage school desk with a chair attached to the desk, and the desktop lifted to reveal all the beautiful supplies of glue, glitter, crayons, sparkles, and anything else you could imagine with scissors and construction paper. Her space had a butterfly wall border a little lower than the traditional chair rail.

We built our new store to our needs. I recall the contractor lowered the light switch in the bathroom, and a peephole was installed at about three feet so my daughter could better utilize the space in the building. We also had a kitchenette with a microwave and fridge, and the George Foreman had come with us. The bathroom was a full bath. That became handy for many things, like the day I stirred the navy-blue screen print ink with a paint stir on a drill and flew ink through the air into my daughter's blonde hair, arms, and legs just before she went to preschool that morning.

We upgraded our screen printer to have six screens available for any given order. The new system also had a conveyor dryer. The dryer was a considerable upgrade to save time and better cure the ink for durability. This printer moved us into the realm of four-color process. Without getting into the science and the color-correct terminology, it's like your inkjet printer; it has magenta, yellow, and cyan-blue inks in addition to black to create all the colors. You need to have those four colors align perfectly to create the effect. Each color is blended as they were printed onto the shirt to produce the result customers wanted. My block letter logo spelling STAMPEDE became filled with a rainbow of color.

The most challenging four-color print we did was for a local '50s style ice cream place. It depicted a pinup-girl-style car hop against a classic car with a tray of ice cream treats. I would like to have thought we would never find the proper mix for that flesh tone. It was amazing when we got them done but a daunting task just the same! That memory popped up on my Facebook the other day. We pulled that off about thirteen years ago, about seven years into the business.

My daughter went with us when the company traveled for on-site printing and vendor shows. She was five years old and very adept at making change. She was overseen, and customers understood the nod to hand over the money. I would attend promotional marketing trade shows. Initially, I was frowned upon for bringing her. However, I assured them that she would be on her best behavior. After that, she was always given a name tag that read "Boss."

When kindergarten rolled around, we had a going away lunch for her last day of "work" before she began full time in the community school district. That fall, customers noticed she wasn't "at work." We worked closely with many customers, creating incredible designs, pulling off last-minute orders, and building many business network connections.

I owned my business and maintained my hours from 10:00 a.m. to 6:00 p.m., making me available to attend school sporting or performance activities for my children. My employees were an integral part of my children's lives. Having dependable employees allowed the extreme flexibility to be present for my children. Christmas concerts, Muffins with Mom, and class activities could be attended without hesitation. If either of my daughters were sick, I could be home with them. The same flexibility was honored for employees and their children as well.

A classic example of attending without hesitation: my daughter was not always a fan of school lunches, but we agreed that school Salisbury steak is just the best. I even discussed the meal with the lunch lady one day while at my store; she said they didn't have it but once a year because of budget constraints. How odd, I thought.

One day I got a call from my daughter while at school. "Mom! Mom, it's Salisbury steak day! I got one for you!"

"I'll be right there!" I replied without hesitation.

I saved the artwork file in progress and dashed out to the school. I spied her right away in the lunchroom. She had gotten an extra Salisbury steak and fork for me.

I sat in the exact middle school cafeteria I had eaten in many years ago. We shared the tray of food, thankful to my business for supporting my family in these tiny moments to be present, illuminating purpose in my path.

When it came time to sell, this was the hard part of the business. I had so many customers that we had amassed. In our thirteen years of business, some had been with me from the start. We supported the local boys' and girls' little leagues in four surrounding communities and our own. We also secured contracts with the local school district and some private schools in neighboring communities. I was never out to take business away from anyone else, but if someone had a new project, I wanted the opportunity to be their new person to meet that need.

As You Reflect On Your Family

What does "family" mean to you? Who are the key members of your family? What roles do they play in your life? What values or qualities are important in your family relationships? How has your family influenced your life and personal growth? Reflect on your ancestors, their stories, and the traditions passed down. How has your family history shaped your identity and values?

Chapter 3

Floatation Therapy, Another Career

How does a human services crisis social worker who has a happy and successful career in graphic design and T-shirt printing in the promotional marketing industry bail ship and find float therapy? That doesn't read like any book should, but it is my life, my story, and what happened.

In high school, I was in two motor vehicle accidents. These accidents occurred six months apart, and in both accidents, I was a front-seat passenger in a car and was T-boned by drivers failing to stop at stop signs. As a result of these accidents, I spent a lot of time in physical therapy that wasn't helping.

The diagnosis of fibromyalgia came in the late 1980s. At this time, fibromyalgia was a bit of a "trash can" term. When nothing would show up on X-rays or blood tests but you had a range of symptoms and syndromes, you were classified as having fibromyalgia. Frequently, this was treated by heavy pain medications, antidepressants, and medications for sleep. These medications may have been part of my high school and college struggles.

However, once doctors handed down a diagnosis, I seemed to get somewhat better. I went through hundreds of dollars in medications each month and was still not pain free. I developed many coping mechanisms to figure out how I could survive with the least amount of pain and still sleep. No, this isn't where I turned to heavy drugs or alcohol. I turned to mind over matter. Most of my tactics were balancing my work and play and getting good sleep and rest.

At this time, fibromyalgia (FM) has been part of my life for twenty-seven years. I functioned pretty well, knowing my limits and managing my self-care. Day to day was okay. Flares were another thing. Pain flares were mainly brought on by overexertion, excessive stress, or changes in the weather. I had a prescription regimen of anti-spasm medicines and anti-inflammatories that worked when the pain was horrible. Insurance did not cover them, and one of them was very limited on how much or how often I could take it due to concerns for liver and kidney function. Weather flares were a whole other thing. The prescriptions were only taken when all else failed. I tried massage and physical therapy, chiropractic adjustments, and osteopathic manipulation, and I modified my diet to exclude foods thought to increase inflammatory conditions.

Then my friend stumbled into REST (Restricted Environment Stimulus Therapy) for FM. There was a study for the effects of floatation therapy on FM. They offered free sessions to get started and discount sessions to complete the ten float study. She told me all about float therapy. "I'm in, of course," I said. The nearest and only float center in Iowa was two hours away.

I knew I was claustrophobic, but I didn't know *how* claustrophobic until the first time I tried float therapy. I took my shower, and I entered that dark Samadhi tank. I remember feeling absolutely petrified, lying on the water in the dark with a washcloth propping the door open just a little bit. I remember lying there and chanting, "If Tracie can do it, I can do it. If Tracie can do it, I can do it!" My heart was pounding like a jackhammer in my chest. My breath sounded like Darth Vader was in there with me. But somehow, I must've chanted to sleep because I woke myself with that funny little whale noise.

My body felt terrific when I exited the tank. Even though I was mentally exhausted, I had to figure out how to return and continue to have these results physically.

I continued to float every week. With each float, I felt better than the float before. The floats added up and felt more compelling and profound, and the claustrophobia became a non-issue. I used self-hypnosis at night to address these fears.

I knew right then that if I could feel better this quickly after twenty-seven years of chronic, debilitating pain, I needed to bring this to my community in southeast Iowa. I set out on building my float center. In our little town, there were many big vacant storefronts.

You need to have some criteria to build a float center. It needs to be able to isolate noise and vibrations away from your float unit; the rooms themselves are soundproof. There was much learning about sound—how it travels and how to stop it.

I went blindly into yet another adventure. We constructed my float center within my mother's family practice office. Her building has undergone many changes in expansion, and a portion was not fully utilized.

While building this float, the fun and enjoyment of the graphic design and promotional marketing was wearing thin. In hindsight, I also saw where other things in my life were crumbling apart. My husband was helping me less and less with the big jobs, leaving me stranded and disappointing customers more often. Looking back, I can see where he, too, was having unrest in his life. During the thirteen years of the graphics business, he had had no fewer than nine different jobs. Our graphics business was very successful, continually supporting our family of four.

I had found a new passion for float therapy. And this only increased and fully intensified when attending the float conferences with all the people from around the globe who were in this beautiful new industry. Competition was not a thing. Everyone was so warm and inviting. Well, of course, they all float! With this modality, I would bring so much relief from physical pain and suffering to individuals who would participate.

My passion for floating only grew, and the graphics business became more of a burden, so I decided to sell it. It was time. I had been there thirteen years, and we had grown the business from so little to so much over that time. I sold the graphics business, and I had more time to pursue promoting my floatation business—my true love, and an industry that also offered me physical and emotional relief from the chronic symptoms of fibromyalgia. I would be a happier, healthier person—a better mom.

What is floating?

How could someone give up so much of what they had accomplished and built to dive off into this passion?

Imagine one thousand pounds of Epsom salt and one hundred gallons of water heated perfectly to skin temperature. The water is about ten inches deep. Once you enter the float unit, you close yourself in it. Yes, that sounds scary. It is not a latch; it's a hydraulic door. It's not a big deal. The water line comes across your forehead, down by your temples, down the sides of your face, and under your chin. It's like you are a face floating there in the water. You reach over and find that button sticking out from the wall, which controls the light within your float unit. Once you turn this light off, all your space issues disappear. You no longer know if you are in a bathtub or a lake.

It is dark, and it is silent. Your body is not physically touching anything. The support of 94.5° water blends with your skin; you are not even aware of the water. You have no signals going into your brain for your brain to be thinking and processing. Your brain is receiving a much-needed rest. There is no cell phone. There is no internet. There is no intrusion in your thoughts. Your brain gets a well-deserved reset and a break. Many studies, including the Navy Seals, use flotation therapy to treat concussions. Many of my clients have had astounding results of the brain fog leaving and their concussions resolving much more quickly with flotation therapy.

As your body is gravity free, all those aching muscles and joints also get relief. They are no longer working to support themselves. You're lying in a giant magnesium bath, absorbing that through your skin. Almost everyone is deficient in magnesium. Sometimes those achy muscles and joints may feel achy during your float. I do not believe it's because they hurt more. I think it is because you have no other processes in your brain and are more aware of them, just like you're more aware of your achiness on Saturday and Sunday when you don't have to rise above it and go to work.

It is an amazing process; if you've never done it, you owe it to yourself to try it. In the industry, we say try it three times; once is a bucket list. After your third float, your body and mind understand how it works and can fully benefit from the experience. My experience in the float industry allowed me to address my physical ailments, aches and pains, and gain control over my chronic symptoms.

Floatation therapy also helps PTSD, anxiety, chronic pain, inflammatory disorders, muscle recovery, muscle memory, and tremendously catalyzes creativity. Ideally, one gets to theta state while floating—the state of lucidness where hypnosis and healing occur. However, many go on to a delta brain wave state and take a great nap.

Floating also allowed me to better connect with myself in my own time and space. We must care for ourselves to realize there is much more to life. For many guests, this is their designated "me time."

Do you make time for yourself? How do you spend your "me time?" Prioritize your self-care by identifying specific self-care activities that align with each dimension of wellness. For example, for physical wellness, you can incorporate daily exercise. For emotional wellness, you could practice mindfulness or meditation. However you do self-care, make it a priority! You can't pour from an empty glass.

Chapter 4

Sales and Marketing, Medical Assistant, and Medical Office Manager

We opened the float center in September 2015, and the business grew. By November, I had a prospective buyer of the Stampede business who had watched the company from afar. They, too, had to make a leap of faith to leave their traditional job and venture out on their own with a young family. The whole process happened rather serendipitously. I did not set out to sell the graphics business. But as my passion for floating grew, it became a more straightforward and natural process.

The sale happened in January. I contracted to continue to stay on with a more part-time nature to transition the business. I wanted the new owners to be as successful as possible. I taught them how to utilize the software, the ins and outs of some customers, and industry-specific terminology. Then, of course, there was introducing my filing system. The computer-based system, the paper order forms, and so forth that I had maintained on all of my clients. That was a huge list! Compiling the customers out of my database to send each of them a letter informing them of the business sale was a significant undertaking. All of the equipment, all of the artwork, and all of the files stayed with the business. I had sold my rights to all the artwork I had compiled in thirteen years.

I had new flexibility that worked well for me and my family, and allowed me to continue promoting the float industry and finish with my graphics customers. Only some people were happy I sold my company. My youngest daughter was disappointed and didn't speak to me for some time. She refused to help move our personal things from the building—a vast part was her toys and numerous childhood memories.

The float business was initially to have opened in June. I had many publications and information encouraging people to explore this new resource. However, there were several construction delays, and we opened on Labor Day weekend in September. I lost my momentum in this process. Note to self: only oversell and promote your product or service once it is in hand and readily available.

Now that the float was open and the graphics business was sold, I was to settle into my new position as a float center operator at my place of business, which was also in my mother's medical practice. Her office also saw some transition then and needed more staff. Inevitably, as I had worked in many roles in her office for the preceding twenty years, I assisted filling in gaps at her office. These gaps always need to be filled.

I found myself becoming more and more involved in the day-to-day business and running of her office. As the float business grew, this was fine. However, as more time passed and more duties were absorbed by me, there was just less to go around and less of me to promote the float business.

I had a solid core of medical knowledge to fulfill many of these duties. Initially, it was just overseeing this or that until an employee was hired to take over that duty. With my presence in the building, that just never seemed to be fully hired out, and I was still in a position to provide for this medical office. This is where pulling together so many parts of my background came together.

Having worked in crisis and my emergency medicine background, triaging patients as they came through the door was easy. We have a significant Amish community in our area, and they appreciated the ability to have minor lacerations and emergencies taken care of in the office rather than presenting to the emergency room.

Our office was the company doctor for area industrial companies too. I had done much triage while working on RAGBRAI and being able to work taking care of wounds on the side of the road, so in the office, this was cake work. I also oversaw supplies and materials for the office and helped with the hiring practices and revisions in an employee handbook. In this office, patients are treated as family. Our duty was to complete prior authorizations for patients to have the needed medications and procedures. I also worked with many patients to help them with prescription assistance programs.

Before this, I had worked with my mom on many outside-of-the-box projects that she had. In addition to being a family practice osteopath, she did Botox, permanent and corrective cosmetics, microdermabrasion, and other procedures I helped her with over the years on nights or weekends. I continued to help with many of those projects, providing consultations and information, and frequently assisting individuals to decide what procedures they were interested in, and what would be in their best interest and most effective for their situation.

Sometimes, we would fall short-staffed, so in addition to being an office manager, receptionist, and insurance clerk, I also filled the role of office nurse. I was taking vitals, drawing blood, and charting appropriately in the medical records, pulling from my past EMT-ID training.

I often worked with patients and their families to help them make educated decisions about their health care, looking into nontraditional medical options as well as seeking the best traditional medicine they could find for their given needs at the time.

I also spent far too much time at the office in this role. There were often floats of an evening, which soon became my sole responsibility. Shortly after the sale of the graphics business, I filed for divorce.

The Divorce

Here I was, the mother of two beautiful daughters. One had just turned twelve and the other would soon be twenty-two. I had just sold my definition of a successful graphic design and promotional marketing business. I had sold this business of thirteen years to pursue my new floatation business fully.

I could write an entire book on the unique circumstances of my divorce. This is not the time or the place. Every story has three sides: my perspective, as I saw the events happening; the view of the other interested party; and finally, the perspective of a disinterested observant party. To this day, I do not fully understand what happened. I did fully see that I could no longer live what felt like such a fragmented personal life.

From the outside looking in, our family had it going on. We had a quaint story and a three-quarter bungalow. We had two dogs and two well-behaved, respected, achieving daughters. We had a thriving business in a small town. We had our classic cars and a beautiful lawn.

I worked diligently to keep this persona alive. Several business startups had happened, trying to replicate my business. We made it all look effortless.

My husband was likely not happy either. As I reflect, I realize that in the thirteen years I maintained a thriving business, he had had no fewer than nine different jobs. Our children were healthy, happy, and well provided for.

The word divorce still makes me cringe. I felt like such an absolute total failure. I hung in as long as possible; I didn't want my children to have a visitation schedule! But I just couldn't do that any longer. The ambitions of only one individual cannot support a marriage. A marriage or relationship takes the active involvement of both parties.

I had spun clear down in life. Yes, I experienced the sudden death of my first husband when I was only twenty-seven years of age, living far from home and family. A divorce was utterly different. While I had the stability of a home and family, I was not prepared to deal with this. I clung to anything that gave me a sense of reality, belonging, and the purpose of being needed.

Divorce was the worst thing I have ever experienced. I felt like my heart had been literally ripped from my chest. It was put into a blender and handed back to me. With the constant expectation that I would just be, I would just be okay.

The youngest, at twelve, was very independent. She often took herself to and from school with her bicycle. We lived close to the dance studio, just over a block away. She was able to take herself to and from dance lessons. The most time we spent together was regularly taking her to the various dance studios that were two hours away. That was when we got to spend time together. The oldest had an apartment and was basically moved out.

In my constant misguided need to have structure and be needed, I became further and further involved in the medical practice. It was taking more and more time from my daughter and my float business. Looking back, I'm unsure how I functioned through any of it, because it is clear that I did not perform to my fullest potential as a mother or a business owner. It was so much easier to be dedicated to the work at the medical office and those patients than to be obligated to my daughter, myself, or my own business.

Transitioning Back into Medicine

Location, location, location…

Following the sale of Stampede Graphics, I was there less and less. Then, when I filed for divorce, I was significantly absent from there.

I was just not able to function in that capacity. Transitioning out of the graphic business was far more emotionally taxing than I thought before I added the complications of divorce. To this day, I miss many of my regular customers. I am ever so thankful to still live in the small community and get to catch up with them now and again.

Being finished with the graphics business logically placed me at the float center full-on with the ability to promote that business. Floatation was such a new territory: the floating industry, while it has been around since the '50s and commercially since the '70s, was still a very new concept here in the Midwest. It was much easier to fall into the role of being needed in the medical practice and not caring for myself, my daughter, or my new unique business.

Getting lost in the familiarity of the medical field was relatively easy, coupled with my innate sense of obligation to help my mother. My daughter at home was becoming increasingly resentful toward me, and our communication broke down significantly. At the time, I attributed much of our relationship to the typical developmental phases she was going through as an adolescent.

Losing myself at work was my defense. Not a tear was ever shed where anyone would know how broken down and lost I had become. A fog that I was unable to see was rolling in. I would have to admit how much of an utter failure I had become to allow anyone, including myself, to see this. I never showed that weakness. I remember pulling into my garage many times, shutting off the car, and lowering the garage door. No one would hear or see me cry alone in silence and seclusion. But only for a moment; I had a child dependent on me. I did not feel I could share that vulnerability with her. I felt obligated always to have my best foot forward and be strong for her. Yes, that silence and seclusion could be found in my float pod, but I could not retreat there for a long time.

This path continued, getting deeper into my own personal dysfunction and disconnection with myself. One day, I looked around my house. The phrase "the apathy train wrecked" sounded in my brain. I remember my stepmother had all the things, all the decorations for all the various seasons. I had long aspired to have them too—different florals for the beautiful lead crystal vase. I had seasonal wall hangings—not just for Christmas. I had achieved that! It allowed me to create a fresh look at home from time to time, to create that feeling of having a new spacious respect for your home, like when you get back from a vacation. I was paralyzed to do anything for myself. Christmas decorations would be coming out soon, but Valentine's was still present. I had lost the ability to fake it at home.

Who was I?
How could I get so lost?
When did the fog get so thick?
How long would this last?
Was it this bad??

"The spirit of Christmas will be here," I told myself. "It will be okay. You'll get out of this funk!" I told myself and heaped the stacks of clutter a little higher and tighter. If I wasn't getting basic floral arrangements changed, I wasn't taking care of anything. I realized this years after the divorce. The pain and spiraling down haunted me for some time. How would I ever be whole again? Was this all there is left to BE-ing?

The Pandemic

When the pandemic hit, it indeed killed my floatation business. The governor of Iowa shut down so many industries. Before this, my floatation business was on track to becoming a thriving business in its fifth year. However, the world was changed for one reason or another. I don't agree with everything that happened during that time. However, I don't know how it could've been done differently. Our society experienced a major upheaval. It created a lot of insecurities on so many levels for all people.

Not much changed in my world; it remained work and home. I was not someone who frequented malls or shopping. Living in a rural area does have its advantages. Such things just are not a luxury here. Our area of the state did not see a rapid rise in cases; overall, we had a very low death toll.

Being full time in the medical office, I was absolutely so physically and emotionally exhausted at the end of each day. I worked diligently to read everything I could get my eyes on and understand and comprehend. I was working closely with public health and understanding what changes and recommendations would come down every day being so different. Our patients looked to our office for the official word on what they should do and how to proceed.

Much changed for my daughter. Schools were closed for the remaining two and a half months of the school year. My daughter's social life was crushed. She was active in early morning weights, dance team, color guard, and marching band before school. She was missing the social busy ins and outs of the school day. The dance studios where she taught dance lessons and participated in her own dance lessons daily after school were closed. She and her friends baked cakes, cookies, and cupcakes for each other. They left packages of their creations on each other's doorsteps, maintaining social distancing protocols. They stayed in contact virtually. We spent more time together, sharing our favorite streamed shows and movies.

Thankfully, a larger dance studio she attended began offering virtual dance lessons. She could participate in virtual classes in my then-vacant commercial building. This opportunity was a lifesaver for her.

As the fatigue of the daily toll of the new pandemic guidelines settled down, a new fatigue arose. The ridiculous stipulations by hospitals regarding who they would see and what surgeries they would conduct impacted my ability to advocate for my patients effectively. Surgeries that I felt were life-threatening were pushed off. I can understand some of it, but medical decisions were not in the best interest of the humans they were trying to serve.

As the pandemic slowed and services were reopened, my floatation business suffered substantially. My float business felt doomed while we stayed busy at the medical practice. People were so scared to resume life. Additionally, so many had significant hardships from not being able to work that they could not afford floats. I offered discounts to bring clients back. I had lost too much ground.

I began to explore other professions, knowing how far I had taken my college education. Having a bachelor of science in psychology meant I had completed many prerequisites to continue formal education in the medical field. I received an official copy of my college transcript. How could I possibly consider re-entering formal education? All those fears of being able to perform well on tests, and read and comprehend well came flooding back. However, I had far more life experience, and I learned how to use the adaptations taught to me at UND to get through day-to-day living. The struggles were not like they had been, but I wasn't taking written tests in real life either.

At this time, I was considering returning to school and becoming a physician's assistant. Looking at what the pandemic had just done to the medical field, how could I possibly even consider furthering my medical education? Anybody that seemed to be within retirement age left the medical field. The medical field was hemorrhaging without enough practitioners to cover the needs of the people.

In researching schools, I learned I must repeat forty of my previously achieved one hundred twenty-nine college credits to apply for acceptance into a physician's assistant program. The colleges mandated that their required classes be taken within five years of your application to their program. I would not be given credit for my life experience or the number of years I had a hands-on working knowledge of medicine.

This just honestly did not feel right. Nor did I think that I had the energy or the interest to repeat forty hours of college credits. I guess I could have taken many courses online. I would have to repeat all those hours before applying to a two- or three-year program, I was looking at a total of five to seven years of education before making a career change. I would be entering the medical field when I was about sixty. That just really didn't make sense.

The process of looking into college made me acutely aware that I was not happy with where things were. The current raging paperwork requirements of human services did not support the joy of making a difference in families. The satisfaction of bringing customers' designs to life with design work didn't outweigh the barrage of demanding customers, and floating made such a difference in my physical and mental health. I resumed many of my hobbies and activities after I developed a regular float practice. But medicine? I love the patients, but it just wasn't my first choice of where to continue my passion.

Where does your satisfaction with your current work fall? Do you have positive boundaries in place between family and work? What, if anything, would you change about your family and work boundaries? What resources would help you make your desired changes?

Chapter 5

Personal Transformation with ThetaHealing®

We now have that silliness out of the way! I had ruled out returning to college based on the cost-benefit ratio. It might be plausible if I had invested all my time in becoming a full-time student. My daughter would soon graduate high school, and my responsibilities were decreasing. I said no. It was time to focus on my flotation business.

While I enjoyed working with patients at the medical office with the fast-paced variety that we had there, it was not my first choice. I wanted my flotation business to be successful. It would take more time and energy to make it happen. At the same time, I was looking at different ways to promote the business. I stumbled onto Alignable. It's like Facebook for business owners.

After I signed up for Alignable, I got a message that said, "Hi Amanda. I'd love to hear about your business," followed by a booking link to schedule the time to discuss our businesses and how we could create referrals to each other. We were both in the alternative healing business, so I thought it was a logical connection. I scheduled a time that we could meet and share our services. From here, I was intrigued and decided to have Dr. Tanya do an intuitive scan. It was very uncomfortable because her virtual intuitive scan's results were spot on and further proved that I was absolutely not happy with where I was, but I saw no way out on my own.

I continued to work weekly to uncover many layers and restructure how I thought, spoke, and saw things. Much of this work was just restructuring my thinking and looking for the positive in *everything*. I know that sounds like total sparkles and fairy dust, but it really does change things. I was taught that whenever I had a negative thought or said something negative, I needed to retract it and send it to God immediately so the negative energy I had just put into the world could be corrected, transmuted, and sent back to the world as peace, love, and harmony. I usually had more of these thoughts or things said while driving alone in the car. I could see myself as a cartoon when I started this practice; anyone going behind me would have been calling in my license plate for littering as I threw so many thoughts and words out the window to be returned in positivity.

I also learned many other skills, such as the emotional freedom technique (EFT), that I could implement immediately and resolve my intense feelings, often anger. I would use EFT to focus on the positive and let go of the negative. It's a method of tapping the twelve meridian points to realign our energy and create a sense of well-being and relief. So much comfort comes from tapping. There's even an app for that! I love using my tapping for so many different things. I use it to start my day off when I feel overwhelmed, and it can help me to put my day to rest and fall asleep quickly.

Dr. Tanya used many other methods with me: Best, ThetaHealing®, Chiropractic, Past Life, you name it, and probably some I don't even know. It worked having a coach to guide me through this process of letting go of all I had stuffed to become more of myself—the person I am meant to be. There were many childhood topics, correcting my relationship with the Creator and accepting and learning that I am a BE-ing of infinite light and love. I still have to remind myself some days.

The best part of so much of this "therapy" is that I did not have to relive the anguish and agony of my story. Yes, there were tearful times, please don't get me wrong. Those times that tears arose, a resolution was completed before our session ended. I left most sessions not recalling all that had been covered but just knowing that I was so much better; I was so much healthier and looking forward to yet another day of positivity.

Dr. Tanya constantly reminded me that I already had this knowledge, saying, "You know in your knower." There were many exercises, journaling, and reading books. These books had a meaning and purpose for me for the first time. I overcame many of the dyslexic struggles and gleaned the knowledge these authors had set forward, understanding how important it is to let go of all of this garbage. All these things were limiting me and my happiness in moving forward—all of these things we hold so deeply and dearly for no good purpose. The beliefs we create around these experiences bring us so much dis-ease, hardship, and illness. Yes, the trapped beliefs limit us from growing and cause dis-ease.

One of the biggest things I learned was letting go of the control aspect. My family had dubbed me as "Cruise Director." I had always done all the research. I knew where we were going and what the possible activities would be, the cost, the schedules, and oh my. We had the best possible outcomes from all of my research. Yes, I love to research.

One time a friend gave me a sticker from a bike rally. It was a helmet sticker, probably one by two and a half inches. It read, in bold letters, "Vicious Power-Hungry B****." I kept that sticker tucked under the cover of my checkbook for years. I always thought "vicious" was an overstatement, but it spoke to my desire to control everything around me. I don't feel I had so much want to control other people, but controlling my surroundings was of utmost importance. I have learned that this need for control is a trauma response. It was limiting beliefs I had subconsciously built to "keep me safe." These beliefs may have had a time and place but often hang on far past their usefulness, where they no longer serve you.

Letting Go of Control

After learning to let go, I vividly recall taking my girls on a family vacation. I knew where we were going; directions were in the GPS. I didn't even get a paper map! I knew where we were staying and when we were checking out. We are all coffee snobs; the youngest had secured where we would have coffee and a splendid breakfast each morning. It was one of the most amazing trips I've ever had. We simply drove along in this very touristy town, and when the girls saw something that looked fun or entertaining, they would call out, "That looks like fun!" to which we would simply pull into the driveway and partake in whatever the activity was. We had no schedule or obligations to anyone but ourselves to have fun. I think it was a fantastic trip. And a lot of learning was done on my part during this trip—learning to let go and enjoy those little tiny moments of celebration and time with my girls.

I continued to work with Tanya for several months. I always looked forward to sessions to gain an understanding of the homework I had completed and more profound learning about myself. I could feel myself waking up. I was bursting out of a shell. I had to fully crack to gain this new respect and appreciation of myself. I was finding the silver lining and restructuring my immediate inner circle. Restructuring my inner circle would be a challenge because many of those closest to me were some of my most significant obstructions to allowing me to grow and fulfill what I needed to do for myself. Much of these fell into the topic of healthy boundaries, setting limits, and teaching myself and others how to treat and hence respect me.

I was getting back the fun me stuffed so deep in the back of some closet, in the furthest corner, of the deepest basement of sludge. Many of those closest to me could see the changes. They wanted to spend more time with me, with the new me. Finding positivity in situations and people is so uplifting. It is uplifting to your spirit and your self-worth.

Think about the last time something trivial happened. What did you see in that? Was it something that happened to you? Can you see how it is merely something that just happened in the universe? Can you find the ability to put a positive spin on it? It was just a trivial event, but this is where it all begins, finding the good in everything. For example, if your coffee spilled onto the saucer, be thankful you had a saucer for your cup to *overflow*. I would take it further and say I was grateful that my saucer was used, and I had a reason to wash it now, not just because it was simply out of the cupboard.

I know, sparkles and fairy dust. As you allow those sparkles and a little bit of that fairy dust into your day every day, each day becomes a better gift. I have another friend who has experienced significant health problems; he's lived a full life. Initially, I didn't fully understand when he said "Every day is Christmas." But think about it; *every day* is *a gift*. It is our gift and responsibility to do something positive every day!

Initially, Tanya told me it would take several months to get me out of that murky basement of sludge and to a happier life. It felt like a death sentence. One: I had to admit that my life had become uncontrollable. Two: I wasn't sure about the financial burden. I agreed to services because I knew I could not continue living like that.

I began working on homework assignments. Some were fundamental and straightforward while other questions needed some soul searching. I had never given myself the freedom to think I could have more than I already had. I somehow had these ingrained values that I was not worth more than what I already had and that these struggles were a consequence I deserved.

People would ask me, "If time and money were no object, where would you go, and what would you do? Where would you live, and who would you be with?" I had no idea that these were actually choices. Choices would take some learning, that I had options. I could *choose* to be stuck no longer!

Of course, much of this comes from the worthiness issue. Many times, I felt I was not worthy. I've restricted myself from so many things by denying my worthiness. I have learned through the work I have done and the training I have taken that we are all worthy. Our stature does not determine our worthiness. This is part of the fact that we are all a Divine expression of love and light. Relearning this and accepting this is monumental. When we allow ourselves to think about being passed up for a promotion as being based on our worthiness, we shortchange ourselves.

My Transformation

To move forward, you need a map. What does your map look like? What does it look like in your new and improved life? You need to have goals and details of what your future looks and feels like.

That's a huge deal—to understand what is holding you back to get there. What keeps you "unworthy" of the greatness you are here to accomplish in this human experience?

We are souls having a human experience and coming into this human existence with knowledge and experiences. That knowledge gets stuffed and overrun with the chatter and clutter of day-to-day life and the indoctrination we go through, not only as children. I needed a coach or a guide to address and assist me in getting back to the experience I came here to have—a coach to remind me of my single path forward.

Of course, this can only occur once you can see your unrest, unhappiness, and genuine desire to change. When I got to that point, the only way out was up. But only after seeing and feeling that I was so utterly alone, feeling trapped without options that had my best interest at heart. It is essential to know that we are here for greatness. I encourage you to look within. Can you see your greatness? Are you ready to seek guidance to a happier, fulfilled you?

I have always been a caretaker; looking out for others was just who I thought I was to be. Only after starting this work did I see that my obligation to always take care of others, without regard for myself, is not the norm. The satisfaction of knowing I had helped was just not enough. It no longer made me whole. I had begun to see and feel the giant hole inside of me.

I was angry! How could so many just take from me? When did I become accepting of being taken from? How did I allow this to keep happening? When did I get this as my worthiness? What beliefs could be trapped so hard to limit me so much?

I had accepted it all—all of the things I learned and internalized as fact. I was the child who was seen and not heard. I was doing as I was told, not questioning authority. I am sure many didn't see me this way. I did have a bit of rebellion in me at times. I was a Gen-X child. During our childhoods, our parents were considered physically and emotionally absent. We were the original "latchkey" children, often caring for ourselves and learning life values as we experienced them. Guessing all the while what is normal.

I needed to address where things seemed to go so wrong and allowed me to feel so worthless. I felt like I deserved all the bad that had come to me. I learned and recovered from so many things I experienced. Recovering seems like a long and arduous task. That sounds like blaming. But actually, in the hands of a gifted spiritual coach, so much happened so quickly.

One by one, these beliefs I knew as hard and fast dissipated. There is no blaming or tracking down where you embedded anything from. But there is honestly looking at everything and deciding what it brings to you. The things that bring you joy, love, and happiness are keepers—examining and understanding those to get more like that to you in all areas. You reap what you sow; being positive brings positivity. It's not all sparkles and fairy dust.

Forgiveness is a huge part. Fully understanding and appreciating everyone for their contributions to your life and know that forgiving is not forgetting. Holding grudges takes away from your joy and peace. It takes a lot of energy too! The most considerable forgiveness is forgiving yourself. We take on so much in this life and are generally our most critical critics. For me, much of my newest anger was at myself. After getting past being angry at what I saw as people taking advantage of me on my way down, I have to take responsibility for allowing that to happen. I did not love and appreciate myself enough to set a better example for how others treated me. My boundaries were lax at best.

Self-love is a vast concept. Many of us struggle with that—loving yourself enough to make changes, improve your life, and create healthy boundaries. This concept sounds simple enough. Trust me, it was a vast body of work to release so many years of entwined limiting beliefs to overcome. ThetaHealing® work was quick and effective.

I had a long list, a journal's worth of forgiveness lists to work through. Forgiving myself for the twisted feelings I had come to have with God. My family, friends, and all the people of the world, it felt like. Forgiveness is a process. I have come to recognize it as more of a process that is ongoing daily. As I worked through these processes, I was happier. I wanted more from life. Following my forgiveness work, I had so much more to give to myself and everyone around me. Letting go of all the weight of anger, grudges, and disappointment clears space for love, caring, and happiness. Purging all the gross binding clutter and allowing in the light.

Chapter 6

Reinforcing Values and Appreciation for Life

Elizabeth Kubler Ross identified the "five stages of grief" as denial, anger, bargaining, depression, and acceptance. This concept first appeared in her 1969 book *On Death and Dying*. These stages apply to any grief or loss you have in your life. The stages come and go, some lasting longer than others, and some we experience more than once.

Much is the same in the steps one goes through to get to a better place. First and foremost for me was addressing the negativity. I could make a list of experiences throughout my life. All of the things that we go through create and build us into the person we are today. Staying in extreme negativity brings on many dis-eases of the body, mind, and spirit. Once you find all of this negativity and release it, you may feel empty. Negativity has consumed so much of your life. Sometimes we must be uncomfortable and vulnerable to get there. We may even need a coach to guide the next step.

As I look at a list of things that have occurred negatively in my life, I also look at the things that I gained from those experiences. I gained adaptability and a larger sense of family. I saw more of the country, experienced great compassion, learned and lived with acceptance, and developed a love of the outdoors. I have learned self-resilience, that I am not alone, but when I am, I can handle it. I have a beautiful home that I can recluse to when needed. I have had diverse careers that have allowed me to work with many amazing people to experience the joys they can obtain. I have two incredible daughters. Did I tell you how proud I am of them?

Many times, when I was identifying a lot of negativity I needed to let go of and venturing into a world of positivity, I found a lot of resistance. It's amazing how comfortable we become in the skin that has grown around us. It is a tough, thick shell, much like a crab's shell, that becomes comfortable until we need to outgrow it. In the process of outgrowing the shell, we show a lot of resistance. What if it takes too long to get another shell of protection? What if I get lost in a new world of opportunity? What if the light is too bright? Who will know me—will I lose the real ME?

Many things that disappoint us in other people are a mirror of ourselves. What annoys you about that lady in front of you at the checkout line? Now truly look. What is it? Is it what she is saying? What is she doing? How is she behaving that annoys you? Now look into yourself and find those characteristics you also participate in. That doesn't feel very good, but it allows you introspection, and you can make changes to be the best human you can be.

The Silver Lining and Forgiveness

So now that we are overcoming our negativities, finding the silver lining in every possible thing, and accepting our resistance as opportunities for change, we need to look even deeper. Deeper is going into that forgiveness. The forgiveness of ourselves, the forgiveness of God, and the forgiveness of all others who have had a hand in how we learned to respond to future events. Forgiveness of all misunderstandings. As we forgive, we thank everyone for contributing to our adventure to make us who we are. So as we are a crab shedding our shells, we can grow and reach new heights in our life along the path.

Be thankful for the adventures and adversities we have had, allowing vulnerability and discomfort as we grow. I often considered myself an excellent example of what not to do. There are worse things in this world. Learning from our experiences is all we can ask of ourselves, and we are making changes by learning—learning discernment to let go and grow from the unpleasantness.

Learning the Magic, Investing in Myself

With my healing and growth, I saw so much and many who were and are hurting as I had been. When the opportunity came to learn the techniques of ThetaHealing®, I was all in. By learning how to implement ThetaHealing®, I could continue to invest in myself and provide healing as I grew. More importantly, I could make this healing available to others as well.

I vividly remember going to the local flea market. It was the fall flea market at the fairgrounds. I had reconnected! I was rounding a significant turn of accomplishment on my journey, and hearing the small limestone gravel at my feet and the feel of the grit in my teeth. The smell of mothballs from storage and maybe a hint of mold. I love antiques. I love touching them and feeling the energy of those who had loved them before!

Oh, I had missed this connection. It is part of being an empath. There are many parts to learning how to use these gifts. It is so daunting many empaths just shut down. It can be so overwhelming to feel all of the energies. Shutting down does feel safest until you learn how to be selective with your connection. Otherwise, it is like the cartoon of the person that can hear everyone else's thoughts, but worse because you do not only know their thoughts, you also feel their feelings. Working through ThetaHealing® allowed me to reconnect to being the gifted empath with appropriate limits and safeties in place. One of the greatest gifts I learned through ThetaHealing® is how to wrangle that inner empath.

I knew I was back in my skin. I was comfortable, and I knew, once again, others needed this opportunity to heal and to be happy. Like me, you must first be ready for change. You don't need to know what that change necessarily is. Just knowing that life is no longer comfortable, you want a change for the better. You are ready and willing to look inward and let go. We have years of getting by and doing for others without regard for ourselves. Can you imagine what it would feel like to wake up thankful and filled with gratitude each day? To love yourself so much that all your needs are met? Your self-care resonates with others. You are more able to care for others, and it brings you joy—no longer taking away from you.

Fully recovering from the past feels and sounds nearly impossible. All that we have become is based on how we got here. The lessons of who we are were learned, deeply internalized, and got stuck as an integral part of us. It is time to place them where they best belong. Send it to God to come back as positivity in all you do. Sparkles and fairy dust again… lighting the path of your journey.

Can you imagine how it would feel to keep the lesson and not have an intense emotional response? How would it feel to keep the lesson and not have any emotional response?

It is said that "time heals all wounds." I feel time creates distance. I think of two significant traumas in my adult life. Before healing, they each hurt to the bitter core. Every time, I would be triggered by a smell, an event, a place, dates on the calendars, a phrase or photographs, and memories. I have many positive memories too that I will forever cherish. These were very painful. They elicited physical and emotional responses. They felt just like the moment it happened. I could see the room I was in when I heard the news and would be taken back to that moment—the panic, the tears, the twisting stomach, the fear, and the need to just scream!

When I engage in public speaking, I often share a straightforward example involving bicycle riding. We've had experiences of wiping out on loose gravel, resulting in scraped knees. After applying a few Band-Aids and receiving some comforting words and gestures for our injuries, we typically get back on our bikes. However, whenever I come across that loose gravel again, there's a reminder—a twinge. I find myself wincing, slowing down, and becoming more cautious. I may even feel the sensation of road rash on my knee as if the accident were happening all over again.

Sometimes, there's a lingering fear that it might happen once more, leading me to make the decision to avoid that particular area. It's intriguing how, before experiencing this pain and trauma, I never really gave that loose gravel a second thought. This situation represents a trauma with a trapped feeling. It doesn't necessarily lead to another accident; instead, it involves the emotions and physical sensations that my subconscious has retained to keep me safe as I navigate through life.

Have you ever encountered a situation in your life where a past experience or trauma continues to affect your decisions and emotions, even when there's no real danger involved?

This is how feelings become trapped beliefs by creating subconscious reactions to all future engagements in your life. With the use of ThetaHealing®, the trauma response is removed. This allows you to have the knowledge of the lesson without the emotional response and obligation. The release of limiting beliefs creates the ability to move forward without old limits.

When my divorce happened, I just became utterly, entirely, and totally lost. Every single thing in my life seemed to be a trigger—a reminder of my feelings of failure. Our youngest daughter was twelve. Caring for her each day and presenting as a stable adult was absolutely exhausting. I knew her world was out of control. Seeing me out of control was just not acceptable at that time.

I hid from all eyes and ears to melt down a little bit here and there. It was nearly impossible to hide the response of being physically ill, wanting more than anything to run away when her dad was coming to pick her up or drop her off. Just knowing he was coming to the driveway made me sick. I didn't need to engage with him. I just knew he would be in such proximity. Running or hiding was not an option; camping out in the bathroom wasn't either. Tears were suppressed too. But as soon as I was alone, the dam would break, and a river of tears and cries of pain flowed. I honestly felt this would never end.

I had become so lost in every single aspect of my life. I could have a beautifully authored grocery list with little checkboxes. I would go into the grocery store, and as soon as I passed through that doorway, I entered a whole other dimensional vortex. It was as if my brain had been sucked out of my head. I had no idea why I was there or what I was supposed to get. Yes, the list was in my hand. The list was not tucked in a wallet or forgotten on the table at home. I still could not function. How could you not shop in a grocery store? What had happened that I had become so lost that I couldn't even pick up the basics of milk, bread, and eggs? I felt like a frequent flyer, and maybe they should've had a revolving door at the grocery store… There were many forgotten items that I would have to go back for time and time again.

My unfounded beliefs about divorce significantly hindered my ability to move forward in any direction. This event was the biggest obstacle in my reality. The accumulation of limiting beliefs created my reality of divorce being the worst thing ever. The beliefs I inherited from my ancestors, fetal development, and all indoctrinations of my life brought me to this point. I have participated in traditional therapy. I conducted therapy in many of my careers to help people have a better life. However, I have found such a calling to ThetaHealing®.

The process allowed me to quickly work through ancestry, past life, and all of this life. I could identify feelings, and from there, I was guided to release them permanently! I can even share space with spiders now that the work has gone to a depth I never conceived.

We now celebrate most holidays as a family again. My ex attends birthday parties at my home and barbecue gatherings at my mother's—all of this at my choice. And to think just a couple of years ago, the thought of him coming to my driveway created a physical illness response. Imagine the freedom of letting go of your limitations to the cellular and DNA levels and celebrating your life once again.

Chapter 7

Learning and Implementing ThetaHealing®

As we embark on the journey of profound self-discovery, we gradually shed the layers of societal conditioning and wholeheartedly embrace the authenticity of our true selves. In this liberating process, we unearth our strength, find our purpose, and allow our voice to resound with newfound clarity and conviction.

So here I am. I am looking for the positive. I am grateful for all that I have and all that is to come to me. I have been implementing new boundaries—many were long overdue. The healing and work I have done has brought me so far! I felt that nothing would hold me back. Self-doubt has been such a constant force to reckon with, and it continues to creep in once in a while. Identifying the doubt and taking corrective steps to continue to work just a bit deeper on that belief empowers me to keep moving forward to a life of purpose.

I have become empowered by the work with my coach and spiritual guide. I learned how I had become stuck, trapped, and unable to move. I was ready to take what felt like the ultimate step—creating a new boundary set in stone. I left my many medical office responsibilities. Life was in an upheaval. There was uncertainty as I took another leap of faith. I was not sure exactly what my future would look like, but it was now *my* future. It would be at *my* discretion to move forward, to persevere in *my* interests, to be accountable to *me*, to establish healthy boundaries, and to teach others how to treat me by respecting and treating myself well!

This was a significant change, and it was scary. I loved and respected myself enough to leave the past behind. I have all the lessons of my history, yet not all the burden and emotional baggage. It required me to maintain my new boundaries and take care of myself. The rearview mirror is small to remind us of our history, and the future is in front of us through the vast front windshield.

I had come to reconnect with my intuition and all it brings into view. Life had a purpose, meaning, and joy. I was not just thankful to wake up each day and do it all again. I had hopes and aspirations beyond the education, a house, a car, and kids!

With this new direction and freedom, I knew I had to learn and share this healing method with everyone. Everyone deserves to be the captain of their life. I've always been active in helping others to their fullest potential. Now I had an opportunity to learn and grow with purposeful knowledge. I experienced my transformational journey, and I knew this method of ThetaHealing® had true merit. I contacted the instructor of ThetaHealing®. She came highly recommended with many years of ThetaHealing®, practice, and teaching. I scheduled a call to discuss the options so I could formally learn and implement this practice to help others.

I learned the next series of classes were starting soon. Oh, I wanted this so much. I used my intuition to connect with God and signed up. Oh, the things we learned! Things we didn't know, we don't know. Each class was a process of clearing negative energy and accumulated beliefs that no longer served my existence. I was enlightened to discover more of myself with each passing class. To be honest, a bit overwhelmed too. We were learning every nook and cranny of our existence.

Even in class, my favorite part of the healing is that I did not ever need to tell my whole story. The lessons occurred over Zoom. As a class of students, we were reminded that we came together in this class as part of God's plan. My classmates and I shared many similar or overlapping limiting beliefs. Our instructor would often say, "There is no mistake in who is in this class." Every day of class contained a common thread. The work we experienced individually rippled to benefit the entire class.

There are fundamental pillars of ThetaHealing®. They go further into deeply held beliefs. ThetaHealing® clears blocks, going to the cellular and DNA levels back seven generations and forward seven more generations. My work has a ripple effect to clear blocks of seven generations before and after me.

So blocks going back generations of bloodlines are cleared for me and help prior generations live fuller lives too. Generations after me will not need to carry these burdens and beliefs either. So my daughter and seven generations will be relieved of the limits I have cleared going forward.

All ThetaHealing® work is with consent or permission. It cannot interfere with an individual's free will. So while the work is finished, some bloodlines may unconsciously hang onto these limiting beliefs. We see individuals hold on to negative beliefs when they have not done the proper clearing to understand how these beliefs no longer serve them.

Classes were eight hours long, leaving one thankful for the hour lunch to process and take a much-needed break. While I often felt tired, there was always a tremendous sense of a weight lifted and the ability to see more clearly to move forward gracefully and easily, often not needing to understand the work at the time it occurred. I could feel the shift and an immediate improvement in my well-being. Working with classmates was incredibly rewarding through sharing the healing with all in the class. Energy work is so powerful. I always said yes to accepting the class's clearing and healing work. I could physically feel most of the shifts.

ThetaHealing® works beyond the conscious level. It works subconsciously to release and replace the limits with whatever is in your highest and best good. On a conscious level, I was often unaware of the work I needed. I would feel the shifts and know work was completed for my highest and best good.

While working in human services in crisis interventions, my experience and education led me to help people. Many times since human services, I have said I need to "put my Susie social worker hat on." But as I trained and used more formal intuitive healing techniques, I realized it was always my intuition. I was recalling what I always knew. I did not learn those things in any classroom. Yes, life experience contributes to how I would initially respond. I saw clear trends of extreme personal bias in the investigative workers of child services as a direct result of their unresolved traumas. I had some myself. I often made different connections with those cases that felt very different and personal.

Working with my clients, I see their a-ha patterns and know it is a divine intervention, not an unboxing of classroom learning. This work is more profound than any classroom. Yes, the classroom and life arenas do teach. The teachings of the classrooms are limited and restrictive.

As an exercise, take a moment to relate. Close your eyes. Breathe deeply and quiet your mind. Now feel how this most recent passage hit you. Eyes closed, deep breath, just BE-ing.

What are you aware of?

Do you remember a time you just knew? You just knew something.

There's that conversation with someone mouthing the words as you speak them. We are all connected. We have common paths. That person you met in line and started a conversation with, longing to know where you know them from or if you will see them again? In my family, we call these ew-ewe-ew moments.

At this time, I have completed the first four prerequisite classes in ThetaHealing® for all other courses. I have also completed the Intuitive Anatomy and Manifesting and Abundance classes. Additionally, I have been a teaching assistant (TA) for those first four classes, going even deeper into my learning and clearing more of the beliefs, and assisting other students in learning this coveted practice as they do the healing.

As part of the learning, my classmates and I trade work frequently. It is incredible to work with individuals who have the same training. These classmates and my instructor have remained close. While healing work can be done on yourself, sometimes, it is not as effective, even if another practitioner only assists me in identifying where the work needs to be addressed.

When you work with me, I bring a toolbox filled with tools and experience to build a lasting bridge in your journey. Working with me will allow you to shorten the many turns and expedite your journey, preventing you from remaining stuck or trapped in a life of just being and not moving forward to your fullest potential.

My services address your pressing concerns. I teach you to use applied kinesiology or muscle testing so you can fully understand the work that needs to be done. More importantly, this skill allows you to know the immediacy of the completed work. Many clients do feel the shifts of energy immediately.

ThetaHealing® work is done in-person or remotely via Zoom or other services. Our work continues to gain momentum and evolve over the coming days. I am not suggesting lifelong services with me. You can return anytime. Services are an investment in yourself to improve your quality of life. I am committed to teaching you how to identify and clear up issues as they arise!

With ThetatHealing®, you do not have to go through and relive past events/trauma/crises/ unpleasantness. However, you do have to move through current issues, feel the emotions of a child leaving home, the death of a loved one, and day-to-day stresses of living. They DO NOT rule how you continue to function. They DO NOT become your identity!

In addition to your presenting complaint, we work to establish healthy boundaries and develop meaningful relationships on Earth, and the depths of your inner strength, power, and courage. As in my previous careers, "Crisis is an opportunity for change." What changes are you looking for? What boundaries are no longer serving you? How can we build a solid bridge in your journey?

Clients feel positive, looking forward to each new day as an opportunity, feeling lighter with clarity of who they are becoming and evolving into. They have more energy and drive to tackle their next adventure in their rediscovered identity as their best self. Fear and doubt are replaced with confidence. Many chronic physical pains and health issues are resolved. Self-imposed limits no longer hold them back from the life they create. Interpersonal relationships improve.

It feels so amazing to get to be ME finally! Living for me and being truer to myself! It is not selfish; I can better give more to others with purpose.

"When you walk into the presence of people who calibrate at the very highest energy levels, just being in their energy field, everything that is diseased or in disharmony is healed. When you bring a higher and a more loving energy to the presence of disorder or disharmony or disease, you are really bringing a healing energy. And that's what healing is involved with: It's no longer allowing yourself to wallow around in a process in which you tell yourself that you don't have the capacity to be able to transcend whatever it is that's bothering you or hurting you or killing you." ~Wayne Dyer

Chapter 8

My Process and Case Studies

Well, there is no right or wrong way to navigate your journey. It must be experienced. I have discovered this in my journey. There are equal right and left turns, creating balance in your life. The objective is to continue to move forward. This is much easier said than done.

As I work with individuals, I see many common threads in the barriers, limits, and blockages we carry in our journey. We tend to carry out obligations in our actions rather than having free will of choice. Many individuals have less-than-valid definitions of trust, fear, and safety. Without having the ultimate Divine Definition and alignment with these concepts in our lives, we tend to go awry, falling into the mass consciousness's definition of that word or feeling, creating erroneous beliefs to live by.

Many clients have struggled with the concept of rejection. Rejection often goes back to the womb or even many generations prior, carrying this rejection forward and having an obligation to be rejected or to cause rejection. In ThetaHealing®, we talk about "having an obligation" in relation to having a belief that does not give you an option; it creates a must-do scenario no matter the effect on yourself.

Countless times in a day, I can't help but think *You don't have to think or live like this* when I observe others. Often, that provokes an instant self-check: "I saw this in another; do I need this work too?" The answer is often yes. It is a challenge not just to blurt out "We can fix this." I know not everyone is ready to believe in themselves, not everyone wants to change. While they don't like where they are, the thought of something different—the unknown—it's just too scary. I get that. But I was so ready, so done with being lost. I was ready to reestablish my identity, my path and to conquer this journey. I was committed to my path and understood it could only lead forward.

When I work with individuals, I empower them to see the limits they carry with them and the barriers it creates, and empower them to overcome these limitations and move forward in their life with all that is in their highest and best good.

In accepting clients, I have a short intake of seven questions—very few details. We focus on what you see as your challenges and setbacks. We look at where you find joy and build your services from here. I've said before I don't need the details; what you need to work on comes through in our sessions. I have some basic tenets that most of us have as limitations in our beliefs that come from mass consciousness. I work with you to release this short list of basic misbeliefs to start everyone on an even playing field. I want to stay focused on what comes up for you. There is no textbook or guide to you that we can follow. You are a unique BE-ing. I only want what is in your highest and best good to allow you a promising future of your creation.

Wor·thi·ness

I thought of myself as worthless most of my life, whether it actually was repeatedly stated to me or just my subconscious internalizing it so deeply. This would only be natural growing up in a time when everyone was busy, always trying harder to be better. Society had created this influx of work ethic that created competition and feeling unimportant, which led me to many of the events in my life being less than satisfying. Worthiness is a common theme among people. We internalize the feeling of worthlessness when we lack discernment in trust, fear, safety, love, and abundance. Working to download and create alignment with the Divine Definitions is a step in the right direction.

Then I work with individuals on the underlying issues, events, or traumas that led to this feeling. Often, I find elements of abandonment, rejection, and traumas that create stuck emotions in my work with individuals. These stuck emotions create a negative loop in the subconscious to protect us from more negativity. While stuck, the subconscious prevents learning from the event and keeps us trapped and enslaved to the negativity we perceive. The subconscious keeps one trapped in the sense of unworthy or not deserving, thereby giving up on having or being more. Once we can alleviate the bottom belief, a person can have that feeling of abundance and go forward in life, being able to receive without guilt and shame.

Examples of Client Experiences

A client in her early seventies was experiencing increased health issues without logical causes. She had participated in traditional therapy for decades. She had dealt with years of trauma, physical and sexual abuse, abandonment, and betrayal by many. In the beginning, we focused on working to create a sense of safety and security where issues could be addressed. Learning many values had been carried forward from generations of beliefs about the roles and responsibilities of a woman. We cleared up anything that arose from the previous session during each session. In turn, it allowed us to work deeper on the beliefs that her subconscious had created.

Much like the spokes of a wheel, each feeling would present itself initially as a broad and large topic. With digging work, journaling, conversations, and intuition, we would find the tiniest of events that created this intrusive belief. Belief work is based on identifying intense feelings rather than needing to explore or relive the difficult trauma. Once identified, the belief was replaced with information for her highest and best good.

This client was saddled with the responsibility of many people from a young age. She served as a surrogate to younger siblings, being the matriarch caring for others in their time of need. She had little to nothing left to care for herself. She was losing her identity and becoming stuck in a negative loop that it always had to be this way. Her medical ailments began to compound and severely limited her ability to live independently. She was losing her independence. Feeling stuck and out of control, this negativity led her to seek my services.

Our work set in to establish and create alignment with the Divine Definitions of safety, trust, fear, and love, how each of them serves her, and letting go of what no longer serves her. This is a common starting point for many. We delved into the most intense feelings that seemed to all but cripple her in the discussion. We worked through steps of forgiveness to herself, her higher power, her family, and many who created, supported, and allowed the events to go unchecked.

Forgiveness is a significant part of healing. There are many negative misconceptions we harbor about forgiveness. I work through these beliefs, letting go of what no longer serves in grudges, punishments, and pain accompanying nonforgiveness. Forgiving ourselves is big. We capture and hold much misinformation as we go through life, often accepting beliefs because of where we encounter them—from those in positions of perceived power over us. I teach my clients how to check in with their higher power—the Creator of All That Is to tap into these proper definitions and create alignment with the true source.

After just a few sessions, she reported having positive self-confidence that she could stand her ground with a family member. She told me about the conversation and how empowered she felt to state her needs and stick within her boundaries—noting that she was not mean or hateful. She said she rather shocked herself in her level of calm. This level of empowerment was monumental.

Our sessions focused on resolving traumas as far back as she could remember. Many sessions were emotional, with tears, anger, and deep feelings. While I do not ask for history, some need to share when I ask for clarity. I watched as the "starting point" of this client's traumas moved forward as sessions progressed. Each week, we identified new areas of beliefs and forgiveness work. She worked deeper and deeper into the layers of her onion and took larger steps through her journey, finding glimmers of hope in her ability to let go of all those beliefs that no longer served her. Her health was improving, as was her desire to resume activities she had enjoyed.

As our session began one day, she abruptly stated her need to look at where she was chronologically. *Let me write down my trauma line!* she thought intently. On this day, her timeline began when she was a late teen. What a mark of accomplishment!

She had an extensively documented history back to fetal development. The beginning of her trauma line had repeatedly been at fetal development in sessions before that day. I also note this is where her forgiveness work ended. She was not ready to address the next stages of her forgiveness timeline. There are many ways to approach forgiveness work. For this client, she chose to work chronologically, starting initially with fetal development. On this day, when she was grappling with knowing the past traumas but not feeling them as intense emotions, her traumatic line began sixteen years from where our work had begun.

In Sessions

As part of sessions, emotions often trigger a physical response. You feel a stitch in your side or a pain in your body. Our work will continue until these sensations abate. I worked with a medical professional who had pain in her side with no known origin. This pain had been present for a couple of months. The pain did not correlate to any internal organs. Perplexed with no relief from this pain, she sought radiological studies; they, too, showed no reason for the pain.

I had the opportunity to work with her. We addressed an emotion that arose with a brief guided meditation to determine the origin of the belief causing the physical pain. She recalled an intense emotion around a specific event in her childhood. The negative beliefs internalized from that specific incident were released in a single session. Her pain went from an eleven to a three on a one to ten scale. The pain stayed gone.

I worked with a young first-time mom. Her labor and delivery went rapidly, especially for a first birth. However, she experienced significant pain and physical trauma in the birth process. She was also struggling to nurse her child. While the lactation consultant was kind, it was just not working. The newborn had not been successful at latching on, and pumping was equally unsuccessful. I worked briefly to clear the birth trauma and forgive herself, her body, her child, God, and all others. Following our session, she returned home and successfully began to pump ample amounts of breast milk easily. She also began nursing with great efficiency.

Having a connection in the medical field, I have received clients with unique diagnoses and less-than-ideal outcomes through Western Medicine. Most frequently, individuals present with unresolved physical pain. Pain medications are not helpful and lead to other complications. Many of these clients present for one session for the initial complaint.

People who are ready for change and aligned with receiving healing make changes quickly. Once identified, we can change the beliefs, align the Divine Definition, and let go of what no longer serves them. The presenting pain dissipates immediately. They move forward with a new outlook that no longer perpetuates the trapped emotions causing the dis-ease and pain.

Another client had undergone several abdominal surgeries throughout her life since childhood. They seemed cyclic. When she presented to me, her pain was so intense that she did not feel she could wait for the next surgery. We set right into work on boundaries and forgiveness. Finding her belief that she needed to be punished for generations of sins by enduring physical pain was pivotal. Obligations to carry her ancestors' beliefs about pain and punishment. This release allowed her to manage pain, not undergo another surgery, and return to work.

Letting Go to Enjoy Your Life

Many individuals can achieve a better quality of life by releasing beliefs and decreasing pain and the effects of dis-ease. Intuitive healing recognizes the mind-body connection and acknowledges that our thoughts and emotions can impact our physical health. By tapping into our intuition, we can gain valuable insights into the root causes of our physical ailments. Intuitive healing techniques can help identify energetic imbalances, release energetic blockages, and promote the body's natural healing abilities. Combining intuitive wisdom with conventional medical practices opens new holistic healing and well-being possibilities. ThetaHealing® does not replace traditional medicine.

Releasing negative beliefs around abundance, success, and failure are powerful tools. I work with individuals and business owners to create and align positive beliefs and feelings toward abundance, allowing them to receive what they manifest. It's much like working with individuals to release the negative beliefs around love and being loved to find their happiness. I have also addressed some unique beliefs that people hold about conception, helping them to release what holds them back from becoming parents of the child they so strongly desire.

I worked with a successful business owner with a large clientele and following. However, she was stuck, unable to continue growing her business. She had started noticing some habits that, while she could see were not in her best interest, she could not move past them. We talked about the things she knew were "wrong." We uncovered the trapped belief and did some work. She felt immediately empowered, ready to move forward, and ready to break the self-limiting ceiling she had inadvertently created. And that she did!—surpassing her goals quickly and efficiently.

My training and experiences allow me to help build your bridge as guided by the Creator. My life experiences have given me much first-hand experience. I, too, thought all this to be "too good to be true" while first experiencing intuitive healing. I have witnessed incredible transformations within myself and my clients. I hope this book has allowed you to see and feel that you are not alone. This is your life, your journey. Many lessons have come and gone. Some were far more remarkable than others. I implore you to look inward and seek assistance in finding a guiding light along your path.

Resources

AmandaBethHealing.com

FaceBook.com/AmandaBethHealing

Instagram.com/AmandaBethHealing

YourDivorceHealing.com

Amanda@AmandaBethHealing.com

Linkedin.com/in/Amanda-Johnson-Iowa

IowaSaltPods.com

Amanda's Inspiring Life

Amanda has had a diverse and remarkable life. She has worked in various fields over the past three decades, including human services, emergency and office medicine, graphic design, and promotional marketing. She has also devoted over 30 years to volunteering with organizations such as the American Red Cross, Hospice, and 4-H, among others. Her commitment to community service is evident throughout her work.

As a mother, Amanda is deeply compassionate and always willing to help others. She has supported local dance studios, music boosters, and other school-related needs. Her unwavering dedication to helping people explore, learn, and achieve their highest goals is a testament to her extraordinary character.

Amanda is also a certified intuitive healer, with six certifications in ThetaHealing. She owns Iowa Salt Pod, southeast Iowa's first wellness flotation spa. Her contributions have been recognized, and she was awarded the prestigious 2023 Geo Ropert Award of Excellence.

Besides her professional and wellness pursuits, Amanda showcases her creativity through crocheting, gardening, and her classic car. Her life is a tapestry of compassion, achievement, and inspiration, leaving an indelible mark on those who have met her. Amanda's journey is a testament to the transformative power of a life dedicated to making a positive impact.

www.ingramcontent.com/pod-product-compliance
Lightning Source LLC
LaVergne TN
LVHW041339200726
843509LV00009B/788